A Planner
and Notebook

for the Studious Student!

Activinotes

Activinotes

DAILY JOURNALS, PLANNERS, NOTEBOOKS AND OTHER BLANK BOOKS

Date/Time	Subject	Activity	Notes

Assignments

Quiz & Tests Schedule

Reminders

Reminders

To do List :

Date/Time	Subject	Activity	Notes

Assignments

Quiz & Tests Schedule

Reminders

Reminders

To do List :

Date/Time	Subject	Activity	Notes

Assignments

Quiz & Tests Schedule

Reminders

Reminders

To do List :

Date/Time	Subject	Activity	Notes

Assignments

Quiz & Tests Schedule

Reminders

Reminders

To do List :

Date/Time	Subject	Activity	Notes

Assignments

Quiz & Tests Schedule

Reminders

Reminders

To do List :

Date/Time	Subject	Activity	Notes

Assignments

Quiz & Tests Schedule

Reminders

Reminders

To do List :

Date/Time	Subject	Activity	Notes

Assignments

Quiz & Tests Schedule

Reminders

Reminders

To do List :

_____
_____
_____
_____
_____
_____
_____
_____
_____
_____
_____
_____
_____
_____
_____
_____
_____
_____
_____
_____
_____
_____
_____
_____
_____

Date/Time	Subject	Activity	Notes

Assignments

Quiz & Tests Schedule

Reminders

Reminders

To do List :

Date/Time	Subject	Activity	Notes

Assignments

Quiz & Tests Schedule

Reminders

Reminders

To do List :

Date/Time	Subject	Activity	Notes

Assignments

Quiz & Tests Schedule

Reminders

Reminders

To do List :

Date/Time	Subject	Activity	Notes

Assignments

Quiz & Tests Schedule

Reminders

Reminders

To do List :

Date/Time	Subject	Activity	Notes

Assignments

Quiz & Tests Schedule

Reminders

Reminders

To do List :

Date/Time	Subject	Activity	Notes

Assignments

Quiz & Tests Schedule

Reminders

Reminders

To do List :

Date/Time	Subject	Activity	Notes

Assignments

Quiz & Tests Schedule

Reminders

Reminders

To do List :

Date/Time	Subject	Activity	Notes

Assignments

Quiz & Tests Schedule

Reminders

Reminders

To do List :

Date/Time	Subject	Activity	Notes

Assignments

Quiz & Tests Schedule

Reminders

Reminders

To do List :

Date/Time	Subject	Activity	Notes

Assignments

Quiz & Tests Schedule

Reminders

Reminders

To do List :

Date/Time	Subject	Activity	Notes

Assignments

Quiz & Tests Schedule

Reminders

Reminders

To do List :

Date/Time	Subject	Activity	Notes

Assignments

Quiz & Tests Schedule

Reminders

Reminders

To do List :

Date/Time	Subject	Activity	Notes

Assignments

Quiz & Tests Schedule

Reminders

Reminders

To do List :

Date/Time	Subject	Activity	Notes

Assignments

Quiz & Tests Schedule

Reminders

Reminders

To do List :

Date/Time	Subject	Activity	Notes

Assignments

Quiz & Tests Schedule

Reminders

Reminders

To do List :

Date/Time	Subject	Activity	Notes

Assignments

Quiz & Tests Schedule

Reminders

Reminders

To do List :

Date/Time	Subject	Activity	Notes

Assignments

Quiz & Tests Schedule

Reminders

Reminders

To do List :

_____
_____
_____
_____
_____
_____
_____
_____
_____
_____
_____
_____
_____
_____
_____
_____
_____
_____
_____
_____
_____
_____
_____

Date/Time	Subject	Activity	Notes

Assignments

Quiz & Tests Schedule

Reminders

Reminders

To do List :

Date/Time	Subject	Activity	Notes

Assignments

Quiz & Tests Schedule

Reminders

Reminders

To do List :

Date/Time	Subject	Activity	Notes

Assignments

Quiz & Tests Schedule

Reminders

Reminders

To do List :

Date/Time	Subject	Activity	Notes

Assignments

Quiz & Tests Schedule

Reminders

Reminders

To do List :

Date/Time	Subject	Activity	Notes

Assignments

Quiz & Tests Schedule

Reminders

Reminders

To do List :

Date/Time	Subject	Activity	Notes

Assignments

Quiz & Tests Schedule

Reminders

Reminders

To do List :

Date/Time	Subject	Activity	Notes

Assignments

Quiz & Tests Schedule

Reminders

Reminders

To do List :

Date/Time	Subject	Activity	Notes

Assignments

Quiz & Tests Schedule

Reminders

Reminders

To do List :

Date/Time	Subject	Activity	Notes

Assignments

Quiz & Tests Schedule

Reminders

Reminders

To do List :

_____
_____
_____
_____
_____
_____
_____
_____
_____
_____
_____
_____
_____
_____
_____
_____
_____
_____
_____
_____
_____
_____
_____
_____
_____

Date/Time	Subject	Activity	Notes

Assignments

Quiz & Tests Schedule

Reminders

Reminders

To do List :

Date/Time	Subject	Activity	Notes

Assignments

Quiz & Tests Schedule

Reminders

Reminders

To do List :

Date/Time	Subject	Activity	Notes

Assignments

Quiz & Tests Schedule

Reminders

Reminders

To do List :

_____
_____
_____
_____
_____
_____
_____
_____
_____
_____
_____
_____
_____
_____
_____
_____
_____
_____
_____
_____
_____
_____
_____
_____

Date/Time	Subject	Activity	Notes

Assignments

Quiz & Tests Schedule

Reminders

Reminders

To do List :

Date/Time	Subject	Activity	Notes

Assignments

Quiz & Tests Schedule

Reminders

Reminders

To do List :

Date/Time	Subject	Activity	Notes

Assignments

Quiz & Tests Schedule

Reminders

Reminders

To do List :

Date/Time	Subject	Activity	Notes

Assignments

Quiz & Tests Schedule

Reminders

Reminders

To do List :

Date/Time	Subject	Activity	Notes

Assignments

Quiz & Tests Schedule

Reminders

Reminders

To do List :

Date/Time	Subject	Activity	Notes

Assignments

Quiz & Tests Schedule

Reminders

Reminders

To do List :

_____
_____
_____
_____
_____
_____
_____
_____
_____
_____
_____
_____
_____
_____
_____
_____
_____
_____
_____
_____
_____
_____
_____

Date/Time	Subject	Activity	Notes

Assignments

Quiz & Tests Schedule

Reminders

Reminders

To do List :

Date/Time	Subject	Activity	Notes

Assignments

Quiz & Tests Schedule

Reminders

Reminders

To do List :

Date/Time	Subject	Activity	Notes

Assignments

Quiz & Tests Schedule

Reminders

Reminders

To do List :

Date/Time	Subject	Activity	Notes

Assignments

Quiz & Tests Schedule

Reminders

Reminders

To do List :

Date/Time	Subject	Activity	Notes

Assignments

Quiz & Tests Schedule

Reminders

Reminders

To do List :

Date/Time	Subject	Activity	Notes

Assignments

Quiz & Tests Schedule

Reminders

Reminders

To do List :

Date/Time	Subject	Activity	Notes

Assignments

Quiz & Tests Schedule

Reminders

Reminders

To do List :

Date/Time	Subject	Activity	Notes

Assignments

Quiz & Tests Schedule

Reminders

Reminders

To do List :

Date/Time	Subject	Activity	Notes

Assignments

Quiz & Tests Schedule

Reminders

Reminders

To do List :

Date/Time	Subject	Activity	Notes

Assignments

Quiz & Tests Schedule

Reminders

Reminders

* 9 7 8 1 6 8 3 2 1 3 5 6 7 *